Books in this series:

# Frog and Dog have a Party

## John Astrop

DERRYDALE BOOKS
New York

1986 edition published by Derrydale Books,
distributed by Crown Publishers, Inc.
225 Park Avenue South
New York, New York 10003

First published in Great Britain by
Beehive Books, an imprint of
Orbis Publishing Limited, London 1986

Printed in Belgium for Imago Publishing Limited
ISBN 0-517-61345-X

All the colors
are mixed up.
Just imagine,
green molasses and
black ice cream!
Can you tell which
colors all of these
things should be ?

**red**
**yellow**
**blue**
**white**
**orange**
**purple**
**black**
**brown**
**pink**
**green**